"After the death of my young daughter, I felt like a raw and open wound. Genesse's poetry was my salve. It gave validation to my pain, and 'The Promise' gave me a reason to go on......"
— Nanette Jacobs, Mill Valley, CA

"My first thought upon reading Genesse's poems, was that every word, every thought written, expressed so perfectly and succinctly the feelings of the bereaved and broken hearted parent! I immersed myself in the beautiful and inspired truth of Genesse's poetry."
— Marianne Lino, The Compassionate Friends, Marin County and San Francisco,CA

"The poems in this beautiful volume touch many facets of the shattering grief and long journey into healing that we who have had a child die encounter. I am grateful to Genesse Gentry for sharing her journey in such a heartfelt, open way. Her wonderful poems continue to help me in my own healing, and I recommend them often, not only to other bereaved parents, but also to anyone who is involved in helping bereaved families."
— Catharine Reeve, journalist and photographer, Berkeley, CA

"I love Genesse's lyrical, intelligent verse. She names the emotions and explains the encounters of her early grief with such honesty and candor that they are instantly recognizable to me...and will be, I suspect, to bereaved mothers everywhere."
— Joyce Andrews, Sugar Land,Texas, National Board Member, The Compassionate Friends, Inc.

"Genesse Gentry's poetry reaches into the deepest recesses of the human heart. In expressing her profound love for her daughter Lori, she portrays a parent's horrific grief experience at the loss of a child. But she also provides us with an astonishing example of a path through the pain and towards a redemption of the spirit. I read these poems over and over again and keep this book right by my bed. It is a deeply beautiful, inspirational book."
— Audre Hallum, Pacifica, CA

"What reached me on many levels about your poems was that they are also prayers; they are soft mirrors of your soul; they are psalms. Using stars as the metaphor at once symbolizes the child - everyone's child - and the spirit love that your poetry sings. You and your poetry have honored us all. Thank you."
—Fred Schaefer, The Compassionate Friends, San Francisco, CA

# Stars in the Deepest Night

# Stars
# in the
# Deepest Night

## After the Death of a Child

Genesse Bourdeau Gentry

Writers Club Press
San Jose · New York · Lincoln · Shanghai

Cover art by Jill Zwicky
Photograph of Lori Gentry by Genesse Gentry
Graphic alteration of photograph by Jill Zwicky

ISBN: 1-893652-43-2

Library of Congress Catalog Card Number: 99-63251


Published by Writers Club Press, an imprint of iUniverse.com, Inc.

iUniverse.com, Inc.
620 North 48th Street
Suite 201
Lincoln NE 68504-3467
www.iuniverse.com

URL: http://www.writersclub.com

This book is dedicated
to
Lori Ann Elizabeth Gentry
2/2/70 - 6/28/91
and to
all bereaved parents
and the families and friends
who love them.

**Lori**

# So She May Hear

Hillside walk
above the sea,
memories, songs,
wash over me.

Every breath
and every thought,
there is no place
where she is not.

Bright sun, blue sky,
so crisp and clear.
I sing my songs,
so she may hear.

Hoping

that these poems will enter your heart
in the spirit in which they were written.

Believing

that they are as close as this novice poet could get
to expressing feelings caused by the death of my child.

Learning

that this journey is the longest, hardest
and most painful of all.

Finding

that with the love and sustenance
of friends and family, grief can be faced,
and from the ashes, a new life created.

Wanting
you to know.

# Table of Contents

# Introduction

On June 28, 1991, our twenty-one year old daughter Lori died in a car accident, leaving our family devastated and crippled by our loss. Her father, Bill, her fifteen year old sister, Megan, and I, her mother, began an interminably long, uphill journey through excruciatingly painful years of grief.

In December 1993, two and one half years after Lori died, phrases, verses, whole poems, began welling up inside of me, wanting, demanding, to be put down on paper. Some of the poems dredged up memories of feelings from the first two years that I hadn't known were still stored deep within me. But a far greater proportion of the poems came to help me describe my feelings as they were occurring then and in the following years. Never having written poetry before, this was truly a gift.

As I tried to express and crystallize the essence of my feelings into words, I began to move more deeply into, and work through, my darkest thoughts and emotions. As I did this, I seemed to be freeing up space for more positive thoughts and feelings to enter my heart and mind as well. From the depths of "finding myself nowhere" in "Freefalling," and hiding in blindness "At the Edge," to the whispered prayer of "So She May Hear," as I allowed myself to feel and express all of my feelings, my slow reconnection to the world began.

The poems come to me now much less frequently. Although I know Lori is always with me in spirit, for the rest of my life I will deeply miss her joyful physical presence. I pray that the poems will continue to come whenever I most need them.

It has been deeply gratifying for me to find that these poems help other bereaved parents and can create little miracles of understanding in the non-bereaved as well. In June of 1995, almost four years after Lori's death, I attended a ten-day walking reunion with a group of women with whom I had regularly walked in 1988-89. Many of the walkers knew of Lori's death. I was given extra-special hugs and told they were very glad I had come, but no one said anything about Lori, or mentioned her death.

1

I had taken the poems with me to share with one special friend. After she had read them, the other walkers in our small Bed & Breakfast group asked to read them too. Conversations sprang up because of the poems, helping bridge the gaps between us, allowing me to become very comfortable with this smaller group. In the larger group, however, unless I brought it up, rarely did anyone ask about my family.

When the walks were over, one of the women asked to keep the poems to finish reading them. A few days after my return to California, very sweet cards and letters began to appear in my mailbox. In different words, various walkers wrote to tell me that they had known about Lori, had not known what to say, and therefore had said nothing. They apologized for this, telling me they now realized that they should have talked with me about Lori and about her death. I was very touched, but completely puzzled. What had happened?

The mystery was solved when, a week later, a letter arrived from the leader of our group. In her letter, she said that, instead of going home like the rest of us, she and five of the walkers had remained together one more night in one of the walker's homes. This is part of what she wrote:

"I think something important happened that last night. Linda shared your poems with us. Your poetry moved all of us to shared tears. The tears came not only from the glimpse of the pain you and your family must live with in losing Lori, but all of us for the first time realized we instinctively have done nothing to help or comfort by not talking with you about Lori."

"Before the walk, many of our group had asked me what to say to you about Lori. I certainly did not know, and said just wait and that you would talk if you felt like it. Now I know that this avoidance just causes you more pain. I am so sorry to be part of it. I had nothing to prepare me to understand. Your poetry helped me to realize how much more you have had to face in the isolation caused by people like me trying to avoid talking about Lori. I hope that you will get your poems published. I think everyone who has had a loss, or has known someone with such a loss, would be moved by reading your poems."

I believe that deep inside all of us is the need to understand and be understood by others. In their own small way, that is just what the poems seem to help us do. Bereaved parents walk long and often lonely roads. Their unbearable grief is often exacerbated by the subsequent loss of relationships with friends and family members who feel unable to cope with the depth, intensity and duration of the bereaved parent's pain and heartache.

If you are a bereaved parent, I hope that these poems will give you solace throughout your own very difficult journey and will help you realize that you are not alone. If you have friends or family members who are bereaved parents, I hope that this book will give you insight and understanding about what your loved ones may be going through. And I hope it will help you find the courage and patience to stand by them in these, their longest, darkest hours. The poems were a gift to me. Thank you for letting me share them with you.

Genesse Gentry
August 1999

## Memento Mori

We hadn't any warning,
the night it all went mad.
We knew not yet of quicksand,
or lives like broken glass.

The day was drenched in beauty,
the mountain sky of blue.
Pine needles had been cleared away,
cabin safe now summer through.

Good food and friends-shared laughter,
planning for the evening's fun,
then officers in the doorway,
bringing news that took the sun.

Telephone calls to parents,
legs like rubber, shaking so,
"How do we tell her sister?
Fifteen, much too young to know."

The long drive down the mountain,
midnight knock in such distress.
When she saw us, she gasped, "Lori?"
crying, hugged her, we said, "Yes."

# The Long Forever

You left us so quickly,
there were no goodbyes.
How long this forever,
your death and our lives.

The sadness, the anger,
the loneliness of three,
preferring four always,
how small, this new we.

# And Yet This Happened to Me

I took motherhood so seriously.
I took nothing for granted.
I was always thankful
for what I had.
And yet this happened to me.

I chose to stay with them,
live through their lives closely,
put my own aspirations
on hold 'til they'd grown.
And still, this happened to me.

My life was spent caring
for two lovely daughters
who made my life special
in so many ways.

One day she was living,
alive, well and thriving.
The next she was gone
to a life we can't share.

I'm learning to struggle
through life and the grieving,
to find ways of being
that bring wholeness and peace,
and live with what happened to me.

## Future Past

Our joyful life,
in memories, past.
The future dead,
horror-cast.

Yesterday held us,
secure and sane.
Today, our tomorrows,
lost in pain.

No bright beginnings.
No dreams to come true.
Just get through today -
just get through, get through.

# My Children

Fiercely, I loved you fiercely,
my first child.
The passion, so much love
centered on one person
eased, flowed into perfection
when your sister was born.

Mother love, so safely unbound
and joyously bestowed upon two.
But my security was an illusion,
for you became our soul child,
too soon on a journey
unshared by our living minds.

And your sister, oh so precious,
I now hold back from loving fiercely.
She who only knew the shared love -
how do I love her now?

Your death brought this numbed protection
against caring far too deeply,
against the terrible vulnerability
of only one living child.

Despite excruciating knowledge
now of all life's possibilities,
will the courage come to let me
open to her love completely
and destroy this fearfilled barrier
between mother and child?

# First Thanksgiving

The thought of being thankful
fills my heart with dread.
They'll all be feigning gladness,
not a word about her said.

These heavy shrouds of blackness
enveloping my soul,
pervasive, throat-catching,
writhe in me, and coil.

I must, I must acknowledge,
just express her name,
so all sitting at the table,
know I'm thankful that she came.

Though she's gone from us forever
and we mourn to see her face,
not one minute of her living,
would her death ever replace.

So I stop the cheerful gathering,
though my voice quivers, quakes,
make a toast to all her living.
That small tribute's all it takes.

# First Christmas

It can't possibly be Christmas
without her being here.
Yet the world is singing round me,
joyful tidings and good cheer.

Though I try to put on armour
and brave the sights and sounds,
a few moments worth of shopping,
and the tears are spilling down.

I pray for strength to do it,
find a path through holidays,
look for shortcuts, good ideas,
some directions through the maze.

Then I find at last the answer:
I'll include her symbolically.
And the giving becomes perfect;
her love's flowing down, through me.

# BitterSweet

Bittersweet journey,
I walk alone.
We took this same path
when last you were home.

I spoke of death then,
not yours, but mine.
You turned the tables -
took cuts in line.

Now it takes courage
to rewalk this path,
to be flooded with feelings,
both joyous and sad.

This wide world of beauty
seems without rhyme or rule,
and the path leads me onward,
through times kind and cruel.

# Why Not Ask Me?

I hear it again and again,
one friend asked another how I've been.
How hard, really, would it be
to pick up the phone and just ask me?

# Good Intentions

I can't stop thinking, feeling,
although you want me to.
My spirit's hurt and bleeding;
it contaminates, seeps through.

How huge the effort taken,
just going to work each day,
trying to concentrate on my tasks,
while keeping tears at bay.

So when I leave the office,
the tears and pain swoop back.
The control I've kept on feelings,
released, tight bars relaxed.

Since evenings are my times to feel,
it's hard to stop again,
put them aside and listen,
to "who did what and when."

It's friendly conversation,
and you wish for me to join,
but in holding back my sadness,
I'm walled off too, from joy.

So I sit and staunch the bleeding
that no one else can see.
As the talk goes on around me,
I disappear quietly.

# Isolation

Protoplasm, amorphous blob,
no energy at all.
Feeling friendless, isolated,
hopeless sorrow towering, tall.

The world goes on, while I'm still back here,
sitting in the gloom.
My life is now an empty picture,
empty walls and empty rooms.

# Freefalling

World crashing,
destroying us.
Life melting,
ashes, dust.

Half of my motherhood,
gone.
Gaping hole in existence,
so wrong.

I thought I would die;
I did.
Wounded, deep inside,
I hid.

No ground beneath,
to stand.
Falling through space,
no land.

Forgetting to breathe,
no air.
Finding myself,
nowhere.

# The Chasm

Screaming in silence.
No one can hear.
My confidence broken,
washed away, drowned by tears.

I can't leap the chasm.
It's too deep and wide.
Your face is in shadow,
no bridge to your side.

I thought that I knew you.
You thought you knew me.
But her death is between us,
and I scream silently.

# Emptiness

All I feel is emptiness
in body, mind and soul.
Nothing possibly could change,
repair me, make me whole.

They say this pain will lessen,
that in time I will find peace,
that these mighty waves of anguish
will someday lighten, cease.

But now their words don't soothe me.
My mind is screaming so.
I can't see reason, meaning.
My bleeding heart cries, "No!"

My life just seems a burden
filled with tragedy and loss
and I cannot make the effort
or pay the price it costs.

They say this pain will lessen.
They talk to me of peace.
But this darkness is so heavy,
my only hope - release.

Will this emptiness devour me?
Existence feels so bleak.
To give my life new meaning,
I know not what to seek.

# Grief

Grief's energy
displaces all else,
fills me with listlessness,
hopelessness,
keeps me from caring
about housework,
about yard work,
about no work.

It is pervasive,
invasive,
corrosive,
and not to be stopped.

It can move in slowly
or quickly
and very slowly moves out,
inch by inch.
Day by day by day
it moves through,
infinitesimally,
letting other feelings,
other thoughts,
imaginings,
even hope,
move in
to replace it
for awhile.

# At the Edge

The chrysalis is gone,
no more protection.
To all the joys of life
there's no connection.

I'm caged behind bars
of my life's making.
My hopes, my dreams,
all breaking.

At the edge of all that's known,
no paths show.
Dusky dimness ahead,
clouds of shadow.

What do I do in this frightening place,
held in its grasp?
Quivering, fragile, my lifeboat slips
away from my past.

How do I discover,
reach new land?
Can I create more castles
on this shifting sand?

How to find and release
what's fluttering inside,
waiting to be born,
yet, in blindness, I hide.

# Nature's Rainbows

We held them in our parent arms
for days or weeks or years.
Now we hold them in our hearts
and cry the darkest tears.

The cord attached to children,
eternally fine and strong.
We never leave the missing;
it holds us all life long.

Our children now inside us -
our souls tattooed with gold.
Their love, their words, caresses,
are hugs that we still hold.

If we open to the knowledge,
that they aren't completely gone,
we will sometimes feel their touching,
sometimes soft and sometimes strong.

When they show us nature's rainbows,
we can feel their proud delight,
sending signs to show they're living,
only far beyond our sight.

# Soul In Translation

Nature, nurture,
and the soul -
not two, but three -
a person, whole.

Sometimes it's smooth,
sometimes frustration,
no simple task,
true soul's translation.

Genetic characteristics,
the circumstances of our lives,
aide us or defeat us,
though the soul transcends, survives.

It's our soul we start and end with,
birth to death, not all, you see.
This life, a loan we're given,
then the soul's again set free.

# Sifting Sand

There seemed a finished edge to you,
a waiting time at hand . . .
a kind of watchful waiting,
an hourglass sifting sand.

You asked me about marriage;
you seemed anxious to move on.
Mother-daughter conversations,
two weeks later you were gone.

Was the wild ride after rainstorm
all a part of some Great Plan?
Or only youthful driving,
music loud and careless hand?

We didn't see the future
to know what life had planned.
Now we're picking up the remnants,
piece by piece and hand by hand.

# Words

Poetic hands,
poetic dreams,
poetic words,
you  gave to me.

Words in lines,
words in phrases,
words that dance
upon the pages.

Words that scream,
words that howl,
words from deep
within my soul.

Words that calm,
words fan the flame.
Words appear
above my name.

Words sing true.
Words mirror thoughts.
Words, secret sounds,
ice cold, then hot.

Words of stone,
words of vapor,
words that skim
across the paper.

Words that once
I, only, knew
now on the page
because of you.

# Memories

Memories fill me,
lodge in my throat,
cover my body,
a sorrow-lined coat.

Layers of melancholy
tears cannot reach
well up inside me,
resisting release.

# Only December

Feelings heavy,
tears and tears.
Will the darkness last?
Or is it -
only December?

Hadn't past months
brought peace and hope?
Where is the strength
of October -
and November?

Lights, carols, ornaments on trees,
cards from friends,
happy times in seasons past.
We remember.
We remember.

Will January bring
light at last?
Will we be stronger then,
for making it through
this December?

When people ask
how I'm doing, I say,
"Well,
you know,
it's December..."

# Skin Deep

I had fun tonight,
but I guess it didn't reach inside.
Now, the feelings rush in,
dark, brooding, heavy,
sadness, so deep.

Like a tremulous smile
that doesn't quite reach the eyes,
the fun didn't break the skin,
didn't reach my heart.

But I'll go out and try again.
One of these times, I know,
something will part the murky barrier,
so that for a while,
joy and peace may wash in.

# Shattered

Shattered.
Mind and body held together
by soul strength,
invisible tape from deep within.

Shattered.
Shards of glass
like a broken windshield,
still holding shape after impact,
but never the same.

Shattered.
All strength pulled to the center,
used for gluing,
holding together what was left.
The first year.

Loss of my child,
a part of my body,
an open wound,
never to heal.

Not enough air in the world to breathe,
just desolation.
All life in shadow of my great pain,
no consolation.

How did I move
through that blackness so heavy?
How did I manage
to move on to now?

In times when anguish
returns full force,
when I feel, as I must,
the hurting renewed,

I have to remember,
take courage now.
I made it those
first years,
somehow.

## Ceaseless Rain

Pit of darkness,
dissolving self,
dark hallway of the soul.

Tear-filled prison,
doing time there.
How to come out halfway whole?

Feeling crazy,
filled with fear,
that the pain will never cease.

How to know
this time so hopeless
is in truth part of release.

Let the tears come,
and the blackness.
Wallow in life's cruelest pain.

Know that sunshine
brings the growing
out of all the winter's rain.

## Secondary Losses

Secondary losses exacerbate the pain
when our children die, leave us adrift,
struggling to stay sane.

Secondary losses - the world, as a safe place
where they would thrive, we'd watch them grow,
now fearful, desolate.

Secondary losses - a friend (or friends) shut off,
can't look at death this closely -
the fear is tempest tossed.

Secondary losses - the ability to cope
with anything and everything
in a world deprived of hope.

Secondary losses - the good things that we held
have lost all their importance
when misery shrouds our cells.

Secondary losses - our laughter, free from care.
The times we see its reason,
delightful, now so rare.

Secondary losses - the ability to deny
that terrible things do happen -
invulnerability, a lie.

Secondary losses - the self-confidence we knew.
Our world view so shattered,
can any part be true?

Secondary losses - the lovely lives we had.
The sunshine that could fill our days,
when rarely we were sad.

Secondary losses
may, transformed, in time come back.
But our children aren't returning.
Nothing, no one, can change that.

# Disconnected

Too weak for holding
to your conversations,
tortured, I tried.

Feeling invisible,
more and more lonely,
pain unacknowledged, denied.

Our friendship's bent
away from closeness.
You won't meet me there.

Good friends must
be open hearted,
sharing, foul or fair.

# Sitting Parallel

You live in a world of external movement.
My world is becoming richly internal.
In my world, people die.
In yours, they don't.
In mine, we live with death,
in the midst of death,
in the memory of death.
You don't, won't, see death,
hear death,
talk death,
remember death.
We sit around a table,
and I am alone.
I feel alone at your table.
At your table I feel most alone.

I have so much inside me,
so much of value, unshared.
You will not see it;
you hide from it, afraid.
You don't realize how good it feels
to be doing this inner work,
to be moving inside myself,
to be moving toward something
bigger than myself,
toward the grandeur of things.
Toward what?
Where am I going?
It's all a mystery
and I am the question mark.

# Unspoken

Dear Friend:  Please put it behind you;
let it go for a while.
You're too lost in mourning;
lighten up, try to smile.
I know it's a tragedy.
I know how you must feel,
but you must just get through it,
move on so you'll heal.
I just can't stand
to see you in pain.
I know if you try
you'll be happy again.

Dear Friend:  The person you still
want me to be
is gone, locked away,
and I don't have the key.
I'm really not choosing
to be like this,
but my life is pure feeling,
clenching me like a fist.
There's a bleak, somber moat
between me and the world,
the drawbridge so heavy,
splintered edges so cruel.
When I venture out strongly,
the pain wraps me still,
colors my actions,
saps at my will.
So please, don't give up,
though I'm hopeless and lost.
Our friendship's true value
reflects in its costs.

# Chance Encounter

Sitting at my table, a stranger, lost in thought,
holding her cup closely until my eye was caught.
She told me of a friend of hers, whose child died months ago,
and that she wanted so to help, but how, she didn't know.

"My friend still seems so fragile; her grieving fills her days.
There must be something I can do, or something I can say."

I looked across the table. Her eyes had filled with tears...
How to answer simply, in words that she could hear.
"I, too, am a grieving mother. I've been there, you could say.
Her hurt is like no other. Have you hugged your friend today?"

"Well, I don't really see her much; time seems to go so fast.
She's always on my mind, but I don't seem to get the chance. . .
And I feel so helpless with her; I can't think what to say.
There's so much changed about her; a stranger in some ways."

"I know you care about her, and I understand your fears,
but her life has been so shattered; her days are filled with tears.
She really needs the contact of you and all her friends
or the walls of isolation will close her sadness in."

She sighed, "I feel so guilty. I've tried in the past, you know.
Her conversations get so strange; I'm not sure where they'll go.
She talks of dreaming visits with her child who's really dead.
I know it's wishful thinking, that it's all just in her head."

"I believe our children do try to show us they live on.
They touch us in so many ways; they aren't completely gone.
Your friend needs you to listen, to show her that you care.
You can't take the pain away, but it will help to have you there."

Continued

"I just wish I could help her. It's just so hard to know..."
She took a breath and let it out and then she rose to go.
"Good luck," I said, before she turned and slowly walked away.
If she will only listen and hug her friend today...

# Fences

I was broken, defeated,
starved for friendship, for care.
I peered out from the shadows
and you were not there.

How would it have hurt you?
What was too dark to see?
What would you have lost
by befriending me?

I'm surviving and learning,
have found friendships true.
And how about you, old friend?
How is it with you?

# The Mystery

They say it is perfection,
no matter how it seems,
in my path through grief's long struggle,
that I'll somehow be redeemed.

I do not feel the choices;
our parts seemed choreographed.
We'd brush against each other.
I'd move this way. You'd move that.

You're in my life for reasons
of growth that I can't see,
and the hurt must be directing
my life's long search for me.

To find what's really in me,
not what I supposed was there,
a journey I've embarked on:
to find myself somewhere.

# Even in the Darkness

My child has died; don't disappear; don't be afraid of me.
I know sometimes being fearful not to hurt, you let me be,
not knowing what to say or do, after unthinkable tragedy.

But when you find the courage and strength to hear my pain,
and listen, really listen, though hidden, there is gain.
The tension built in silence, if released, can keep me sane.

Let me talk or not talk; let me laugh or cry.
Let me be just how I am; let me shout to God, "Oh, why?!"

By pretending nothing's happened, to ease my mind that way,
instead, it builds such pressure, I hear nothing that you say.
But if you truly let me show the pain and loss I hide,
the tension lessens and retreats. Your words can come inside.

If you can, please call or visit, at least one time per week.
(The time you find is flying by, to me just seems to creep.)
I cherish the flowers you offer, the small gifts and the cards.
They show me that you love me, know it is so hard.

I don't need from you life's answers,
and you can't stop the pain from the loss.
You can't make me "forget it,"
get back to the way I was.

But helping through my grieving,
our bond will surely grow,
and where it all will take us,
none of us can know.

Continued

Please let your heart stay open,
unafraid to share my plight,
so you may be beside me,
when this darkness burns to light.

No

I can't make small talk anymore.
My interest wanes; no gain I see.
I try to remain focused
when it doesn't interest me,
but it takes so much effort.
I resent the heavy fee.

Yes

The cherished talk I'm drawn to's
heart to heart and soul to soul.
We discuss the thoughts and issues
in our lives as they unfold,
our two halves of conversation,
warm and friendly, filling holes.

# Sharing

Today, my friend, we chanced to meet
and tears were in your eyes.
You'd just been to the grave side
of my daughter, who had died.

From your saddened visage,
clear, again, it was to see
you also loved my daughter,
and you cried for her, and me.

This accidental meeting
helped connect us through our tears.
Lori's spirit shines within us;
in our friendship, she appears.

## You Listen, Still

Tonight we cried together,
my lovely, special friend.
It's rare to share true feelings;
most try to keep them in.

When all my words are sad ones,
and all my thoughts tear-filled,
it helps to know you love me,
enough to listen, still.

Others think to cheer me
they should take my thoughts away.
But my pain remains unbroken.
My words dam up and stay.

Instead you burst me open -
out come my words of grief.
I share my darkest thoughts with you,
and then I feel relief.

# Gold

Beginning after high school,
we've remained close through the years.
How valued, now, your friendship.
You're undaunted by my tears.

Your loving, gentle presence
in my life through these hard times
has given me perspective
and hope for peace of mind.

Amidst the pain and anguish,
you help me to survive.
Our cherished times together
are treasures in my life.

You smile on me like sunshine.
I share my thoughts with you,
get strength from you, and wisdom,
an uncommon friend, and true.

Your courageous understanding
takes in my deepest pain.
With love, total acceptance,
you help me breathe again.

# Two Families

We've always shared the fun times,
our families, yours and mine.
When tragedy struck at our house,
you remained a true lifeline.

You took turns protecting;
camping magic helped each time.
The care that you each gave us
felt like God's graceful sign.

Together we remember
her laugh and sense of fun,
the way she had of saying things,
the woman she'd become.

We remember thongs at snow line,
the card games, playful noise,
the younger girls following on the beach,
sneaking up on her and BOYS.

She'd a special bond with Sara;
they'd hang, as two buds will.
I know that true affection's
a bond between them still.

She watches o'er our families,
as you've watched over us,
sending her love from heaven.
That now must be enough.

# Companions

After her death,
I only felt
like a zombie in my skin.

Then you'd come,
with something fun,
take me into the world again.

Walks in the hills
or on the beach
helped me find some hope.

Cafe mochas,
mystery teas,
talking, helped me cope.

Camping sunsets,
sharing books,
there's no one else like you.

This I know,
when the chi does flow,
it will be because of you.

# William

My partner on life's journey,
we've truly been lost souls,
losing all perspective,
thrown up against the shoals.

We thought we had the future
bright before us shining fine,
then life lost all its meaning
in a fateful twist of time.

We've been holding on together,
keeping company, yet alone.
We've felt the grief so deeply,
it has scarred our very bones.

The support that you keep giving
is in letting me just be,
never angry or complaining,
so that I can refind me.

## California Window

Darkening, lowering rainclouds,
sights that bring to me,
thoughts of deep contentment,
fireside, books and tea.

To quietly gaze and listen
to the wind and pouring rain,
roaring, louder, louder,
then more softly, soft again.

Here we're blessed,
four seasons sun,
but when the cloudbursts
finally come,
rainsong quenches,
eases pain.
My dry soul
soaks in the rain.

At end of storm, crisp sunlight,
the world fresh and washed clean.
I breathe in all the beauty,
crystal colors, satin sheen.

I walk the joyous hillsides,
my senses sharp and free;
the deepest well, I'm finding,
its source bubbling now in me.

## Smiling

I could feel you smiling
as I opened the book today.
It felt like, "Good for you, Mom.
This will help you on your way."

I love that small connection,
of knowing that you're there.
It's such a special feeling,
a rainbow I can wear.

# Choices

Morning sunlight, swaying daffodils,
signaling winter's end.
*My Son, My Son*, the book before me,
Iris Bolton, author, friend.

Up for tea. Through kitchen window,
finch flailing seeds around.
Always before, irritation, the feeder empty,
seeds on the ground.

But as I watch, observe more closely,
now a new thought seems to grow.
I filled the feeder; my gift was proffered.
Now my claim on it must go.

The seeds are now in his possession;
their care not mine to question how.
How like the lives we gave our children,
they promised not, nor took a vow.

The gifts of life and love we offered.
What they did, their choice to make.
Lovestrings attached to all our giving,
their choices caused our hearts to break.

Now back to Iris. I read on.
Page 62 comes next.
There in print, my thoughts exactly,
she's put down in words, expressed.

How magic is this thought connection,
over time and over space.
Our children died, but we're still living,
ideas shared, life's simple grace.

## Spring Sorrow

The world with beauty
seems to fill
this time of evening
calm and still.
Runners, walkers
share with me,
partaking of
this majesty.

The greatest pain
no longer felt,
released by earthly
sights and smells.
By walking,
walking,
with the dog,
the tears still flow -
but gone the fog.

# Sand and Sea

Hawk soaring, floating free,
blue heron watches, silently.

Songbirds, celebrating spring,
green lushness, over everything.

Ahead we hear the roaring waves.
I've longed for this sound for days.

Poppies next to buttercups,
the sand dune's there, ahead of us.

Cliffs of white, deserted beach,
free at last, at ocean's reach.

Aquamarine, cerulean blue,
life's secret source must hide in you.

I breathe in deeply, salty air;
the breeze blows sweetly, 'gainst my hair.

Sandpipers in surf. The tide is out.
Sadie lurks, then routes them out.

Sunday morning sand and sea...
God's smiling on this place and me.

## Hound's Tongue

Spirit-hued dog,
my sympathy,
you walk along
the path with me.
You run ahead,
then stop and turn,
wade through creeks,
among the ferns.
You chase the birds
and squirrels too.
I follow, on
this walk with you.

Morning sunlight
through the trees,
a sense of peace
comes over me.
The beauty of
this springtime scene
creates a place
of harmony.

Miner's lettuce,
blue-eyed grass,
butterflies flit
as we walk past.
Shooting stars,
'neath sky of blue.
We walk the path.
I think of you.

# My Friend

You were my friend,
not my child only.
Your life cut short,
mine doubly lonely.

You'd share with me
both tears and laughter;
no more such talks
from here-on-after.

There are great holes
where you have been,
just memories now,
of you and then.

# Searching Through the Darkness

The days seem darker,
nights more hushed.
Before, your laughter
lightened us.

Your quickness caught
each humorous flash.
Much now escapes,
eludes our grasp.

How can we bring
that spark so bright
back to our lives
without your light?

What were the tricks
that made you see
how much of life
ran joyously?

# Returning

Everywhere
a trace of you.
Nowhere now
the face of you.

Laughter
only echoes.
Sad embers flame
like bellows.

Each memory place
too dear to face,
without you.

# On The Other Hand

On one hand,
you have died; you're gone.
On the other hand,
I feel your essence, know you live on.

On one hand,
I'm drowning, see the abyss.
On the other hand,
you make contact, send eternity's kiss.

On one hand,
I grieve, lose hope miserably.
On the other hand,
your happiness comes through to me.

On one hand,
I'm so hurt, broken apart.
On the other hand,
you're connected straight to my heart.

Yes, I do understand
you are happy and free.
I'm not crying for you, now,
I'm crying for me.

## June's Gift

Gladiolus rising
from nowhere
so it seems.

Tall and magic flower
vivid crimson,
just a dream?

No one planted;
no one nourished,
but somehow it appeared.

A symbol
of your gladness
in this sad, sad time of year.

# The Wedding

## Katie's Getting Married

We're going to the wedding;
you would want us to.
One bridesmaid will be missing
and the pain will pierce us through.

But Katie's getting married.
Such a friend was she.
You can't attend in body,
but spirit, hopefully.

Will she sense your gladness
and know you're with her too?
She'll walk the aisle in beauty.
May she feel your love shine through.

# The Wedding II

## This Is Lori's Mother

On the way, came panic. How could I get through this?
Lori, not a bridesmaid. Oh, how she'll be missed!

I held the tears 'til sitting. "Should we leave?" he asked.
"No, I just need to cry," and slowly the tears passed.

The bride was oh, so beautiful, the groom cute as could be.
Lovely bridesmaid, Heather, and my smile came easily.

My wink at Katie passing, smile changed to seriousness.
We together thought of Lori, her absent conspicuousness.

Was she here now with us? No sign, but I just knew.
She sent her love from heaven, and Katie knew it too.

At the reception after, no expectations, I just went.
I was treated with such honor, the warmness fills me yet.

I was "Lori's mother" again for that one day.
no one afraid to say her name, introducing me that way.

Three years and they still speak of her to friends she'd never met.
How joyfully I learned from them how much she's thought of yet.

I remained 'til all were leaving, basking in the glow -
a day being Lori's mother - beyond her death, love's flow.

## Surviving

There's no way to know,
in those first, early years,
if the crying will stop,
be an ending to tears.

But slowly, so slowly,
through the grieving and time,
will come moments and days,
when hopefulness shines.

Backwards and forwards,
into darkness, then out,
we begin to start living;
scraps of new life peek out.

This happens most surely,
survivors will tell,
when we find time for others
and give of ourselves.

## You Touch Us Still

Fair and lovely
woman-child,
of royal waves
and flashing smiles,
your life though ended,
you touch us still.
You come when needed;
our thoughts you fill.

Your angel presence
in our lives
brings rainless rainbows,
sunset skies,
shooting stars,
visits in dreams,
visions and music -
gifts, unforeseen.

## Stages

When she died, the numbness
encased my broken heart -
nothing could pierce the center
to break the grief apart.

I'd feel others' tragedies
with an added sense of gloom,
but for empathetic sadness,
there seemed no longer room.

Now the morning paper
brings the world inside.
I can feel its joys and sorrows.
My heart no longer hides.

# How Will It Be?

Three years of holidays have gone.
How will this one be?
It's now mid-November,
blue sky, gold, russet leaves.

The second year almost as hard
as the first, in memory,
and last year with its dark descent,
brought me poetry.

What will year's end bring this time?
Just celebrations' mire?
Or will the love surrounding strong
bring peace to damp the fire?

## Dark When All Is Light

Sing no more of holidays,
now that she is dead.
Without her flaming presence,
our spirits, lined with lead.

The laughter, joys, of days gone by
are shadowed now with gloom -
the silent house, so sad, so sad,
the tears that fill each room.

We wish so to escape this time,
but her sister still is here.
So we go through all the motions,
and get through it this year.

# Candles in the Night

Candles flame in darkness,
flicker, steadily glow,
bringing light from shadows
and help to soothe me so.

My daughter, like the candles,
gave my life true light.
I use the candle's beacon
to connect us in the night.

As I light the candles,
my wish and my request
is that she'll see my signal
and know my love's expressed.

As her light joins my lights,
our worlds touch and flame.
As I snuff out the candles,
I softly say her name.

## Empty Places

I drove the old way yesterday.
It'd been a while, you see.
And there, without a warning,
the pain washed over me.

I drove the old way yesterday
and sadness came on strong,
taken back by so much feeling,
since you've been gone so long.

Places seem to lie in wait
to summon up the tears,
to say remember yesterday,
those days when you were here.

Places where you laughed and played
are places where I cry.
These places hold the memories
that will live as long as I.

## Your Birthday

The daffodils are coming up,
but you're not here.
The hills are turning green again,
and you're not here.

The days are getting longer;
Groundhog Day is near -
your birthday - you'd be 25,
but you're not here.

We think we are accustomed
to the fact that you are gone.
Then here it is - your birthday -
and the memories come on.

Tears of joy and happiness
twenty five years ago -
so precious and so tiny,
we delighted in you so.

Your sunny, smiling presence
brought happy childhood days,
and fun with other children,
with your sharing, caring ways.

Trusting turned to shyness,
brought on by days at school,
learning that there was a world
where sometimes friends were cruel.

Continued

Wanting a world of fairness,
frustrated when things weren't right,
a playful spirit and funny,
you hated unjust slights.

You had soft strength and beauty
and loves that lasted long.
Sardonic wit, light hearted ways,
made love for you so strong.

Europe brought the laughter
we hoped would never end,
but life said "No, that's now enough,"
and brought us home again.

Our relationships had strengthened:
a family - yet good friends.
You'd visit us from college
and the laughter would start in.

Your years slipped by to twenty
and then to twenty-one -
a car ride on a rainy road,
and then your life was done.

And soon your birthday - 25,
should be a banner year.
What will we do to celebrate,
when you're not here?

Thoughts of you, most surely
will fill us all the day.
Will we feel you close, or just the loss -
knife's edge, or rainbow's ray?

The days are getting longer;
Groundhog Day is near.
Your birthday - you'd be 25,
but you're not here.

## Dear God,

It is said: When one door closes,
another opens.
Is this so?

It is said: It's all a balance,
equal good with equal bad?
Do they know?

What happens when they leave us,
those who brought us peace and light,
and lost to earth the starshine
that so brightened up the night?

Does the light somewhere extinguished
for a time create a space,
'til the goodness pulls together
and is somewhere else replaced?

Can all the pain and heartache
that is cast up by the void
in the end be transmutated,
into peace and into joy?

Did the closing doors in our room
shift the axis, move the tides?
Will the night-time burst wide open,
and refill our starless skies?

## On the Wings of Butterflies and Angels

On the wings of butterflies and angels,
I stay above the quicksand and the strife
remembering to notice all the magic
that comes seemingly unbidden to my life.

With their help, I feel the strength of starlight,
know sunshine's mixed with shadows great and small,
know instinctively the path that I am treading
will eventually lead somewhere after all.

In easy times their blessings float down clearly
in a serendipitous, radiant flow;
at other times, when blindness claims my vision,
I have to find the trust inside my soul.

But they are all ways and forever trying to show me,
give me signs that they are with me in my plight.
I must watch for subtle or kaleidoscopic colors
and listen . . .
for the gossamer winged whisper of their flight.

## Suffering and Wonder

Her death left a firestorm of destruction
and desolation in its wake—
ashes, our lives blackened, twisted stumps,
burnt free of superfluity,
dead to life, to joy, full of
smoke and shadow-covered dreams.

"Suffering is the base of happiness," Thich Nhat Hanh says.
"You can learn from your suffering. And then
you have a chance to be happy. But if you don't
know anything about suffering, I don't think
happiness can be real and deep."

Today I am happy; I know that I have suffered,
and I will suffer more because of my daughter's death.
That layering of suffering and grief is boundless,
both nourishing me and holding me back. At times
I succumb to its heavy weight, making me feel lethargic—
the slow creep of molasses in my mind and body,
the downward drag of her death instead of
the upward flying wonder of her life.

At other times, like now, I know that I am healing,
that new shoots are coming up through blackened ground
and that from dead-looking stumps is sprouting new life.
I feel the nourishing, budding aspect
that suffering and grief have brought to open me
to parts of myself unknown to me ever before her death.

In these times, I know her presence as so much more
in spirit than ever could have been in life.  Though I
long to touch and hold her with my physical being,
I instead hold her with my heart and mind and feel
the new growth poke through the tear-filled soil
and find that it is mixed with angel's dust.

## Supplication

December, you force false gaiety upon our world,
celebrations, parties, the holiday habits of cheer.
December, you shroud us in old memories,
pain and sadness so consistently each year.

I would forgive you, December, for the magic of the past
that  you try every year to bring back,
but your coming ends another year without her.
In your demands, we feel so sharply who we lack.

Please help me, dear December, to forgive you;
maybe in this way the pain will ease.
In forgiving you, December, may I open to your gifts
and the lovely, soaring promise of your peace.

## Grief's Garden

When our innocence has ended
and the dark night has begun,
despair and heartache vie with numbness,
mind and body, shocked, unstrung.

Levels of pain and understanding
must be reached ere we see gain.
Taking longer than expected,
no one else can know the pain.

Grief, like clearing virgin farmland,
full of boulders, stumps and stones,
back breaking and bone crushing,
and, in great part, done alone.

Think when feeling strong emotion,
"Another boulder moved today."
When it's felt with all your being,
it can then be moved away.

If we feel the stone's not moving,
we may have to look beneath,
bring to sunlight what's in darkness,
so what's there may be released.

Treat yourself to gifts and blessings
that will help to keep you strong.
Give yourself to happy moments,
feel each feeling, then move on.

continued

Work and work to clear the garden,
feel transcendence in the toil.
Under all the stones and boulders
will be found much fertile soil.

Watered by our weary weeping,
warmed by tender words and sighs,
green shoots sprouting all around us,
springtime comes through open eyes.

When we look to find what's growing,
we are shocked to see ourselves.
Now replacing fearsome chaos,
an awakening garden dwells.

- - - - - - - - - - - -

As at first we glimpse the garden,
the next moment it feels gone.
It's a painful kind of growing,
falling back, then moving on.

Since this garden's fed by feelings,
some form mist to block the view.
If we try to feel them wholly,
they will always move on through.

Just when we think we're finished,
that the hardest work is done,
there before us, weeds and brambles,
so immense they shade the sun.

Grief's garden work's not easy.
But from deep inside the soul
will come strength and deep compassion.
With love and care it will take hold.

And our children watch the growing;
somewhere they are growing too.
And the tears that flood the garden
create rainbows and clear views.

With our gardens we pay tribute
to our children who have gone.
Their memorials are our gardens;
through our gardens they live on.

## The Promise

Your birth brought me starshine,
the moon and the sun;
my wishes, dreams gathered
'round my little one.

My life became sacred,
full of promise and light,
all wrapped in the girl-child
who brought love at first sight.

The years of your living
filled with laughter and tears,
excitement, adventure,
some boredom, some fears,

but ended too quickly,
ahead of its time.
The loss so horrendous,
such heartbreak was mine.

But from the beginning,
one thought rose so clear:
never would your death erase
the years that you were here.

I would not be defeated
or diminished by your death;
I would hang on, learn to conquer,
if it took my every breath.

For if your death destroyed my life,
made both our lives a waste,
'twould deny your life's meaning
and all the love you gave.

I vowed that years of sadness
would change, with work and grace,
to years of happiness, even joy,
in which you'd have a place.

Memories of you, like shining stars
in the patterns of my soul,
are beacons flashing light and love,
and with them I am whole.

In your honor, I live my life,
now living it for two.
Through all my life, you too will live.
You lived, you live, you do.

## Aquarius Child

Sparkles of star dust
born with the sun,
Aquarius child,
amethyst one.

Golden curls dancing
or still in my arms -
lap-snuggling sweetness,
storybook charmed.

Flowers and firelight,
laughter and love,
calmness and storm clouds,
magic and hugs,

butterflies, angels,
a song in the night,
sunsets and rainbows,
an egret in flight,

rain on the rooftop,
ocean in storm,
ancient oak's mystery,
a dog curled up warm,

stars shooting towards us,
sky crimson, scarlet, gold,
the softness of kittens,
the pure icy cold

of mountains in winter,
silence, snow deep,
castles and fairy tales,
a baby in sleep.

All this and more
you, who came with the sun.
Aquarius child,
dear amethyst one. . .

## Stars in the Deepest Night

When life held
no light or texture,
and I was burdened down
by grief,

when an aching,
purple bruising,
carried pain
without relief,

when descent
seemed most persuasive,
when the will for life
seemed lost,

when the dark
was most pervasive,
midst the numbing
pain of loss,

came the touches
from my daughter,
came the knowledge
of her life,

came the loved ones
to sustain me,
came words wondrous,
burning bright,

sparks to light
the path before me
helping warm
the coldest night.

When Lori died, her sister Megan, our younger daughter,
was only fifteen.

## Megan

You hold our love in your hands
as your life keeps ours flowing into the future.
Your love and life's adventures
help plant us in the present,
instead of in the past.

You are grace and beauty.
You are light and joy.
You are a world filled with sunshine.

You, who were always part of two,
deprived of sister-ness so young,
now finding your own dreams,
building your own life,
on your own terms.

As our living hands hold and release,
hold and release you,
sisterly love and encouragement
rain down upon you,
joining her light with yours,
all your life long.

These next two poems were written by Megan.

## Dying Young

As the seasons change,
time fades away,
the trees to brown,
the sky to grey.

Our feelings change
as life goes on.
Only memories remain.
All else is gone.

Now we stare,
pray to the moonlit sky,
dream and wish
for one final goodbye.

The whispering wind
and each shooting star
call your name
so near, yet far.

The songbird dies;
its last song not sung.
These sweet refrains:
ode to dying young.

Megan Gentry
1991
(Age 15)

# Her Voice Remains

I dreamt, or thought I heard you
through songs of whispering trees,
through winter's solemn slumber
and autumn's eternal breeze.

And through the air a voice rang out
and sought me for my ear,
wanting so to tell a tale
that dreamers only hear.

She sang about life's springtime,
of winter, summer, fall,
of all the change and cycles
that create us, one and all.

She asked me why I sat and cried
or longed for all that's gone,
or hurt and pained for stages past,
or wished the deer, a fawn.

I answered that it hurt me
to lose so much I'd gained
or find I'd lost complete control
of all the life I'd tamed.

And yet, she sighed, you realize
this life is not our own;
we take a part, we do our best
and leave the rest alone.

The storybook has opened
and you have graced a page,
and only will the story end
when life's lessons come of age.

And do not think your duty past
when death comes to your door.
Young lady, you have tales to tell
and stories still in store.

And with this soothing promise
she left me to this life,
to walk with new found knowledge
and loose my inner strife.

And yes, I know the name of you
through bird or wind or rain
who came to me with love so wise
to soothe my inner pain.

Megan Gentry
1994

# Acknowledgments

The death of a child completely destroys the fabric of a parent's life. Before my daughter Lori died, I was a very independent person with many friends. After she died, I lost my sense of self, my ability to think straight, to find the energy for anything besides the bare necessities of trying to function in my job and relate to my husband and surviving daughter, and crying.

My friends were used to my self-sufficiency and leadership and didn't know how to deal with this role reversal. Not knowing how to help me, I was in many ways left alone. I very much needed to talk with my friends, in order to process what was going on inside of me, but did not know how to let them know how much I needed them.

Thankfully, over time, some old friends and many new ones came into my life. I would like to express my gratitude to those people who, in their varied, unique and marvelous ways, have been so important to me since the death of my daughter Lori.

***Cathy Hicks, whose care and friendship provided the strongest and warmest light in my very darkest hours, and for whom the poem "You Listen, Still" was written.

***Jill Zwicky, who designed the cover for this book, and for whom "Gold" was written.

***Ewa Jansson, for whom "Companions" was written.

***The Compassionate Friends (TCF), a support group for families who have experienced the death of a child. The friends we have made in TCF are some of the most important and beloved people in our lives. I receive so many blessings from my continuing participation in The Compassionate Friends.

***The Jansson family, Lars, Ewa, Karin and Sara, for whom "Two Families" was written.

***Carol Whitmire, Louise Hubal and Julie Dietz who joined me in discovering new paths in our beloved Marin County hills, thus enabling me to absorb the healing that regular exercise, beautiful scenery and deep conversation can bring.

***Ellae Elinwood, whose special wisdom inspired "Grief's Garden."

***Carolyn Ryan, the leader of our walking group for allowing me to use her wonderful letter in the introduction.

***Family members and the following friends who have acknowledged Lori's birthday and the anniversary of her death over the years: Birgitta von Frenckell, Louise Hubal, Cathy Hicks, Jill Zwicky, Liliane Matar, Kathy Fitting, Mary Gorman, Christine Morgan, Kathy Lowrey and Carole Wright. And those people, especially Lori's friends, who still talk about her and tell me how much she is remembered, and how much she is missed.

***Joyce Andrews, Kitty Reeve, Georgia Alioto, Marianne Lino, Louise and Bruce Hubal, and other bereaved parents for having faith in me and this book of poetry and insisting that I get it published. And to The Compassionate Friends editors who have used many of these poems in their newsletters and in the national TCF magazine, *We Need Not Walk Alone.*

***My family, a constant source of love and memories—my parents, Cledith and Helen Bourdeau; Bill's parents, Ed and Marie Gentry; my brothers, Walt, Ed, John and Joe Bourdeau and their families. And finally, my husband Bill and our precious daughter Megan, whose presence, love, patience and understanding have been indispensable blessings in my life. The poem "William" was written for Bill and "Megan" for Megan. I would also like to thank Megan for allowing me to include her two beautiful poems in this book.

***Lori, dearest older daughter, none of these poems would have been written, if not for the heartbreak of missing you. Thank you for the gifts your life has given us and for the love you send.

Thank you. Thank you, dearest friends and family. You are indeed my shining stars.

Genesse Gentry
June 1999